EDITION

POWER
Struggles

Successful
Techniques
for Educators

Solution Tree | Press

a division of
Solution Tree

555 North Morton Street
Bloomington, IN 47404

800.733.6786 (toll free) / 812.336.7700
FAX: 812.336.7790

email: info@solution-tree.com
solution-tree.com

Printed in the United States of America

20 19 18 17 16   5

Library of Congress Cataloging-in-Publication Data

Mendler, Allen N.

  Power struggles : successful techniques for educators / Allen N. Mendler, Brian D. Mendler. -- 2nd ed.

     p. cm.

  ISBN 978-1-935543-20-6 (perfect bound) -- ISBN 978-1-935543-21-3 (library edition) 1. School discipline. 2. Classroom management. 3. Problem children--Behavior modification. 4. Teacher-student relationships. 5. Control (Psychology) I. Mendler, Brian D. II. Title.

  LB3011.M43 2012

  371.102'3--dc23

                    2011027054

Solution Tree
Jeffrey C. Jones, CEO & President

Solution Tree Press
President: Douglas M. Rife
Publisher: Robert D. Clouse
Vice President of Production: Gretchen Knapp
Managing Production Editor: Caroline Wise
Copy Editor: Rachel Rosolina
Cover and Text Designer: Jenn Taylor

For the thousands of talented, tireless educators who make differences in the lives of students every day and receive too little appreciation. On behalf of hostile, aggressive, difficult to reach youngsters, thank you for not giving up.

—Allen Mendler

To my wife, Renee, for unconditional patience, guidance, support and love. You are an incredible teacher, person and my best friend. I am so lucky to have you in my life. I love you.

—Brian Mendler

Acknowledgments

I would like to thank Rick Curwin, my friend, colleague, and frequent coauthor for his helpful suggestions in editing this manuscript. A special thanks to Gretchen Knapp and Rachel Rosolina at Solution Tree for their in-house editing. I want to thank the wonderful folks at the Teacher Learning Center for their support and collegiality: consultants Willeta Corbett, Jerry Evanski, and Colleen and David Zawadzki; program manager Jon Crabbe; and office staff Allison and Erin. My wife and fellow educator, Barbara Mendler, has always been a wonderful sounding board and frequent adviser. Her "it's about the kids" philosophy has helped many educators and has always influenced my work. I also want to acknowledge my three extraordinary children—Jason, Brian, and Lisa—and their significant others—Ticia, Renee, and Zach. I am extremely proud of you, as you each are making the world a better place for those who are less fortunate. It has been particularly special to collaborate professionally with my son Brian on this book and several other projects. It is not every father who has the opportunity to watch his child take his life's work to a whole new level. You are doing that in your own way. Finally, my grandchildren Ava, Caleb, and Megan: I thank you for the unconditional love you give your "Papa." It is hard to find the words to describe the endless joy I feel when I am around you.

—Allen N. Mendler

Thanks to the following educators who continue to utilize our work on a daily basis. We appreciate the support and continue to be amazed at the dedication you show your students on a daily basis.

Amy Allega
ELA and Social Studies Teacher
Cleveland, OH

Pat Billone
Fourth-Grade Teacher
Greece, NY

Julee Boeshart
Director of Curriculum
Bellevue, NE

Brenda Boyd
Welch, WV

Stacey Braley
School Counselor
Holley, NY

Carolyn Campbell
Special Education Teacher
Rochester, NY

Sandra Carroll
High School Teacher
Holley, NY

Tom Chaffins
Supervisor of Secondary
  Education
Princeton, WV

Sue Cory
Principal
Holley, NY

Michael Costa
Physical Education Teacher
Rochester, NY

Stephen Eagles
Junior Principal
Sao Paulo, Brazil

Joe Eno
Dropout Prevention Coordinator
Smithfield, NC

Jessica Evans
Special Education Teacher
Buffalo, NY

Carolyn Falin
Assistant Superintendent
Welch, WV

Martin Garza
Principal
Houston, TX

Marcus Hartel
Special Education Teacher
Penfield, NY

Brian P. Heffron
High School English Teacher
Romulus, NY

Michele Heiderman
Special Education Teacher
Akron, NY

Anne Marie Holland
Special Education Teacher
Lyndonville, NY

Jennifer Hopkins
High School English Teacher
Eaton, OH

Jessica Humphrey
Intervention Specialist
Cleveland, OH

TroyAnne Huntington
Special Education Teacher
Franklinville, NY

Jennifer James
Second-Grade Teacher
Cleveland, OH

Carolyn Jarvis
Behavioral Specialist
Barre, VT

Ann Kelly
12:1:1 Grades 1 and 2
Utica, NY

Janice Klinzing
12:1:1
Medina, NY

Jim MacKinnon
Staff Development Specialist
Dorval, Quebec, Canada

Kerry Macko
Assistant Principal
Henrietta, NY

Sheila Madore
Spanish Teacher
Akron, NY

Mike Marra
Seventh-Grade Teacher
Syracuse, NY

Holly Martin
Special Education Improvement
  Specialist
LeRoy, NY

Rae Lynn McCarthy
Special Education Improvement
  Specialist
LeRoy, NY

Marcy Prado Cuevas
JR. HS SPED
Santa Rosa, TX

Marcie Richmond
Director of Special Education
Olean, NY

Karri Schiavone
Director of Special Programs
Holley, NY

Lori Skelton
Non-District Specialist
Rochester, NY

Sylvia Sklar
McGill University Center for
  Educational Leadership
Montreal, Quebec, Canada

Matt Slavik
Biology Teacher
Jay County, IN

David Triggs
CEO of Academies Enterprise
  Trust
England

Shelby L. Webster
AIS Reading
Mt. Morris and Wayland, NY

Solution Tree would like to thank the following reviewers:

Jack Decker
Instructional Support Program Coordinator
Lower Macungie Middle School
Emmaus, PA

Jeannette Goins
Social Studies and Science Teacher
Carroll Middle School
Raleigh, NC

Rory Mack
Reading Teacher
East High School
Laramie, WY

Phil Ruetz
Special Education Teacher
Evergreen Elementary School
Casa Grande, AZ

Table of Contents

About the Authors

 **Allen N. Mendler**, PhD, has worked extensively with children of all ages in general and special education settings. An experienced educator and school psychologist, he has consulted for many schools, as well as day and residential centers throughout the world, providing training on classroom management, discipline, and best practices for motivating difficult students. His work focuses on developing effective frameworks and strategies for educators, youth professionals, and parents to help youth at risk succeed.

An accomplished author, Allen's titles include *Motivating Students Who Don't Care*; *Connecting With Students*; *What Do I Do When . . . ?*; *MORE What Do I Do When . . . ?*; and *Handling Difficult Parents*. He coauthored *Discipline With Dignity* and *Discipline With Dignity for Challenging Youth* with Richard L. Curwin. His latest video set, *The Four Keys to Effective Classroom and Behavior Management*, which he developed with Curwin and Brian Mendler, won the 2007 Association of Educational Publishers Distinguished Achievement Award in School/Class Management Technology. In addition to his books and staff development programs, Allen has published articles in *Educational Leadership*, *Reclaiming Children and Youth*, and *Parenting*.

An acclaimed presenter, Allen has presented for such educational organizations as the Teacher Learning Center, Discipline Associates, Phi Delta Kappa, the Association for Supervision and Curriculum Development, and Reclaiming Children and Youth. His Discipline With Dignity program was made the official program of the New York State United Teachers. Training and workshops on this program have been provided to tens of thousands of educators in schools throughout North America, Europe, Japan, and Israel.

Allen earned his undergraduate degree in psychology and education from Queens College, master's degree in psychology from Alfred University, and doctorate in school psychology from Union Graduate School.

 **Brian D. Mendler** is president of the Teacher Learning Center and is a highly sought-after consultant. The strategies he shares with K–12 teachers and administrators are practical and timely, and most importantly, they work with difficult and disruptive students. Brian has extensive experience working with challenging students in general education, self-contained, and inclusion classrooms. He is also an adjunct professor at St. John Fisher College in Rochester, New York, where he teaches behavior management and introductory special education classes.

Brian's book *Tips 4 Teachers* is an easy-to-read, practical resource that provides educators with specific strategies from the Discipline With Dignity approach to behavior management. Brian is also the author of *The Taming of the Crew* and is coauthor, with Richard Curwin and Allen Mendler, of *Discipline With Dignity, 3rd edition*, and *Strategies for Successful Classroom Management*. In addition, Brian contributed to the video program *The Four Keys to Effective Classroom and Behavior Management* featuring Curwin and Allen Mendler.

Brian graduated from the State University of New York at Fredonia with majors in communication and video production and minors in English and journalism. He earned a master's degree from D'Youville College in Buffalo, New York. Brian is a volunteer for the

Big Brothers Big Sisters program and for Special Olympics track-and-field and softball programs.

Visit Allen and Brian Mendler's Teacher Learning Center website, www.tlc-sems.com, for more tips and strategies.

To book Allen or Brian for professional development, contact pd@solution-tree.com.

Introduction to the Second Edition

Inappropriate behavior that leads to power struggles consumes too much instructional time in too many classrooms. Minor disruptions quickly escalate into classroom battles, eroding relationships and respect. This practical handbook is designed to provide the busy educator with specific strategies of prevention so that power struggles occur less often. By understanding what motivates students to challenge the teacher's authority, it is often quite possible to get ahead of the curve by interacting with the most difficult students in ways that will make them want to behave. This book will show you how. It also includes easy-to-learn methods of intervention that take little time and that maintain the teacher's authority and the student's dignity.

This second edition offers many new strategies of prevention and intervention, tweaks some of the strategies from the original to make their use even more effective, and adds more details as well as examples to make this volume even more user-friendly. Since the emphasis of this book is on practical strategies, there is a relative absence of the guiding theoretical framework. Interested educators can refer to several of our prior publications, which are listed in the references and resources.

When Kids Push Our Buttons

At six years old, Curtis is already a handful. He is often out of his seat, doesn't do much of his work, and likes to bully others. He is at his worst in the least supervised places like the cafeteria, hallway, and playground. When told what to do, he rarely complies. Ms. Lane has called home several times, taken recess away, changed his seat numerous times, and used stars and stickers to little avail. The color-coded (red, yellow, green) system of discipline that works for most of the "good" kids does little to influence Curtis. He misbehaves his way to "red" by 10:00 a.m. most days and therefore loses privileges.

Devon, Sherry, and Latoya are older and text their friends rather than focus on the lesson. Mrs. Martin tells each of them to put away their phones. Within seconds, they are back at it. Mrs. Martin warns that she will take the phones away, but Devon tells her that she has no right to do that. She reminds him that she is the teacher and therefore has every right to take it. Unafraid, he continues his defiance, and Mrs. Martin eventually sends him to the principal. Sherry and Latoya comply for a moment, but as soon as Mrs. Martin's back is turned, they begin texting again. Meanwhile, Julio has his head down on his desk. When called on, he has no idea what is going on and says, "This is stupid." Carl tells him to shut up, after which Samantha tells Carl to shut up. These skirmishes go on for several minutes interspersed with an occasional reference to the day's lesson.

Just as things have settled down, Devon walks back in unaccompanied from the office. Although he seemed to see the error of his ways with the principal and promised to be good upon returning to class, he continues right where he left off. He makes noises and funny faces while waving his cell phone. Exasperated, Mrs. Martin resumes her efforts to gain control with minimal success.

Next door, Ms. Highland welcomes a new student to her special education resource class. Jermaine recently returned home after living in a group home for a year due to a number of problems, including active displays of hostility toward authority figures. On his first day, Jermaine is distantly quiet in class as Ms. Highland leads an academic discussion. Toward the very end of class, Ms. Highland attempts to engage him.

She says, "Jermaine, because you're a new student in our class, I am interested in hearing any thoughts, ideas, or impressions you have of our class."

Jermaine stares ahead; then, without changing expression, he looks directly at Ms. Highland and says, "I think this class sucks!" Some students become intensely quiet as they await Ms. Highland's response, while others take on more of a "What are you going to do about it?" posture.

Ms. Highland takes a few deep breaths, scratches her head, looks directly at Jermaine, and says matter-of-factly, "Jermaine, there may be some truth to that. Maybe after class, you can tell me how you think things could get better here. Thanks for speaking your mind." Unrattled, she deftly redirects the class back to the lesson.

After class, she meets with Jermaine, asks him a bit about what led him to his opinion, and then lets him know that, in the future, she would appreciate him sharing his specific thoughts in a more appropriate way. She gives him an example of how he could let her know in the future. She says, "Jermaine, I might be a little old fashioned, but just so you know, I am way more likely to listen when I hear words like 'I didn't like the class' or 'I thought it was boring' rather than 'This class sucks.' Now what was it that turned you off?"

Jermaine shares a few details and without any prompting, he apologizes.

Although most students who misbehave and escalate a power struggle are almost always struggling with issues unrelated to the problem at hand, how we respond to the challenging moment and what we do afterward can strongly affect whether or not these problems continue, get worse, or improve. Too often, behaviors like Curtis's and those of Mrs. Martin's students exhaust the teacher and erode the classroom climate needed for success. While not all challenging moments end as successfully as Jermaine and Ms. Highland's, there are many things educators can learn to say and do to defuse power struggles effectively. This book offers a variety of specific ways of doing just that.

> **How we respond to the challenging moment and what we do afterward can strongly affect whether or not these problems continue, get worse, or improve.**

Preparing for Power Struggles

We estimate that 70 to 80 percent of challenging student behavior is primarily attributable to factors outside the school, such as dysfunctional families, unsupportive parents, inability to see how success at school will matter in life, violence in society, the effects of drugs and alcohol, a culture that too often values fast and easy solutions, and fragmented communities. While teachers are rarely the root cause of these behaviors, there is much we can do to keep these behaviors from occurring or escalating in our classrooms.

Power struggles develop when students refuse to follow the rules, fail to accept a consequence, or follow the rules and even accept the consequences, but do so with an attitude. Some students are actively defiant and challenge authority at every turn, while others are quietly hostile, like those who refuse to talk or do their work.

Although passive-aggressive students can be frustrating to work with, the authority of the educator is most obviously challenged by students who are verbally and actively challenging. Not only is a power struggle occurring between the teacher and student, but a classroom full of onlookers (students) usually watches every move. Most educators feel angry when students push their buttons, and they let their anger take hold by pushing back. While giving in to the fight-or-flight response is understandable, doing so only serves

Many teachers report the following forms of verbal defiance from their students:

- You can't make me!

- You're not my mother!

- Whatever!

- No!

- When are we going to ever use this?

- This class is boring.

- That's stupid.

- This class sucks!

- My mama will _____.

Examples of nonverbal active defiance include:

- Continuously coming in late

- Making noises

- Flipping off the teacher (middle finger raised)

- Smirking

- Throwing things

- Sitting slouched or with arms crossed

- Bothering others

to escalate the situation, leading to a no-win outcome. Typically, the final move used by the teacher is to either isolate the student in time-out or send the student to the office. Rarely do these solutions work.

Unfortunately, teachers are set up on day one at a huge disadvantage in numbers. In most classrooms, there are at least twenty-five students but only one teacher. However, great discipline and classroom management can level the playing field, and every teacher can learn these skills and defuse power struggles before they begin. These skills will be effective year after year, because students are extremely predictable. The faces change every year, but the behaviors remain the same. This is a good thing! In addition, teaching is one of the most predictable professions in the entire world. Think about it. We know the exact days of the week we are going to work, the exact times we are going to work, and the exact place we are going to be. In what other profession do the customers (students) return every single day even if the product (teaching and curriculum) isn't viewed as satisfactory? We teachers have more control and knowledge than we sometimes realize; we gain wisdom through our experience working with all kinds of students.

Knowing what difficult students are going to do before they do it helps us prepare a response to their challenges. A power struggle is similar to a bad storm—doesn't it end up being much worse when you didn't know it was coming? When properly prepared with food, shelter, and maybe a good book or new release, the storm can actually become a break from the daily grind. When a teacher is properly prepared with the right strategies, inappropriate student behavior can actually present an opportunity to teach and show students how and why they are expected to behave. We will provide you with strategies to help keep the storm away. Just as importantly, though, we will show you how to forecast and understand which supplies to keep with you and use in case the storm hits. Part of this prediction stems from understanding root causes of behavior.

Understanding Why and How Students Misbehave

Understanding the *why* behind misbehavior is key in figuring out what needs to be done to fix it. Think of the behavior (calling you names, throwing a chair, not sitting still) as a stomachache. A stomachache is usually a symptom of something else: overeating, food poisoning, flu. If you take an antacid, the symptom might go away for a short period of time, but the condition might get worse. When we understand the root cause of a behavior, we can tailor the "medicine" to fit the individual issues.

Fortunately, there are highly predictable categories that help us understand why students misbehave. They include the need for:

- Attention
- Power or control

- Competence

- Belonging

Memorize these reasons, and you will quickly be able to dissect the root cause of a misbehavior, which will allow you to figure out the proper strategy to fix the problem.

Attention

There are two types of attention-seeking kids. The first type gets little if any attention at home or elsewhere. In his mind, bad attention is better than no attention. He acts out because then people notice him. Being the disruptive kid has become his identity. What do you do? Shower him with attention for doing anything well—and we mean *anything*. Walking into a class correctly, making eye contact, having a good twenty minutes . . . praise him like crazy, but be sure to do it privately. Public praising turns off a lot of difficult kids because many feel they have to act cool to save face with their peers, while others may think you are trying to manipulate them to be "good" more often. When he acts out, he needs to be ignored. This will be difficult, but remember the root of his problem is the desire for attention. Do not waver; only give attention for positive behaviors that you want to encourage.

The second type of attention-seeking kid gets too much attention at home. She usually has parents who make excuses for her. She is coddled and spoiled. She goes to bed when she wants, eats what she wants, and rarely has to share anything. Once she's old enough, she comes to school. School is all about doing everything she has never had to do at home: wait in line, take turns, say please and thank you, raise her hand. She must learn to live without constant attention and instant gratification. Offering a positive challenge usually works better with this student. For example, a teacher might say to a student who hates standing in line, "Just about anybody can complain about not getting his or her way. Not everyone is able to take turns. I guess we'll see if you have what it takes!" Notice how the symptom (the desire for attention) is the same, but the medicine is different.

Power or Control

All humans want to feel like they have some influence and control in their lives. In fact, a lot of rigorous research confirms that the feeling of control—the belief that you have the power to influence and shape even small aspects of your fate—can have an enormous impact on one's well-being. In a classic study, Langer and Rodin (1976) found that patients in nursing homes who were given small choices about such things as which nights to attend movies, what time to have their meals, and how to arrange their furniture not only engaged in more recreational activities than patients without these choices, but they had a 50 percent lower death rate at an eighteen-month follow-up. Much of our research (Curwin, Mendler, & Mendler, 2008) has shown that when students are given a voice in developing and modifying classroom rules, they are much more apt to follow those rules as opposed to rules developed only by the teacher.

School is often not set up for giving or sharing control, however. Students are told what to do, when to do it, and how long they have to get it done. Giving students a sense of control is especially important when you want to change their behaviors. After all, students make the decision to act out or not. We have seen various attempts at encouraging student engagement in changing their behaviors. When we visited a school in Arkansas, for example, an elementary teacher used a "boat system" to try to modify student behavior. Down the left-hand side of a big chart on the wall, each student's name was written on a cardboard cut-out boat. Across the top were three different categories: your boat was smooth sailing, your boat was in rocky water, or your ship had sunk!

> **Giving students a sense of control is especially important when you want to change their behaviors.**

The teacher asked what we thought about her system. Our first question was, "Who moves the boat?" Not who literally moves the cardboard cut-out, but who decides when the boat moves from one column to another? If the student has a say in deciding, we like the boat system much more than if the teacher decides on her own. Most kids seeking power want to have a say in what happens to them.

Our second question was, "What happens when a student's boat sinks?" Does the student drown, or does she get another boat? Is she given another boat, or does she have to do something to earn one? Our recommendation was for the teacher to meet individually with students and try to come to an agreement about where both she and the student think the boat should be. If the boat had sunk or was in danger of sinking, she should elicit a plan from the student to "right the ship." Students who are seeking power or control need to learn and practice better ways of influencing the events and people around them than by acting out.

Competence

The final two reasons students misbehave are tied directly to how well they perform on a daily basis in school. People need to believe they can master a challenge in order to access the effort and determination necessary for success. Kids who don't understand what is going on in the classroom are like tourists in a foreign country who don't know the language. Unless an interpreter is present, they feel lost and confused. School is set up for some students to succeed; many are able to sit still, pay attention, follow directions, and memorize information for tests and quizzes. Others may be very smart, but not school smart. Unfortunately, since they think they are not smart enough to succeed, they may mask their inadequacy by acting out or pretending not to care.

Belonging

Most students have a strong need to feel connected. Some naturally get this need met because they connect well to the curriculum, the teacher, and other kids who do well at school. Others may belong to a sports team, musical group, or religious organization. For some students who do poorly academically or do not belong to any positive group, however, belonging is directly tied to disrupting class. They want to feel part of a group, so they seek others like them who feel disconnected—others who have given up, or are giving up, on the idea that they can succeed in school.

Preparing Students for How You Will Handle Misbehavior

Preventing the storm begins with teachers telling their students what to expect before the bad weather hits. Let students know that you will respond to every infraction, but perhaps not at the moment it occurs; that you will offer private words of praise or correction on occasion, and that these are between you and the individual student; that you will differentiate instruction based on needs; and that you welcome their feedback on how you can be the best teacher they've ever had. Following are a number of different prevention phrases guaranteed to help significantly reduce the severity of power struggles. Many power struggles start over issues of consequences, fairness, embarrassment, and being told what to do. Unlike a script that actors might be expected to follow verbatim, these are offered as examples for handling such issues. You need to phrase things in a manner that is comfortable for you. Expect excellent results if your phrase captures the essence of the examples that follow.

Following Up Later

Frequency: Preferably said on the first day of school or early in the school year, and repeated regularly until students understand.

Prevention Phrase:
Unfortunately, some of you in this class might do and say some rude, nasty, inappropriate, or mean things. I know this because it has happened almost every year I've been a teacher. I just want to let you all know right now that if and when it happens, I will not always be stopping our lesson to deal with it. It doesn't mean I didn't hear or see it, because I probably did. There isn't too much I miss. It also doesn't mean I am going to ignore it, because there is a very good chance I will address it. I believe in consequences, and there will be consequences in this classroom this year. Sometimes I just think teaching is more important in that

moment, so I will continue with the lesson, and I will expect you all to continue to learn. I might decide to wait until later to deal with the student, because I will usually not allow one inappropriate behavior to get in the way of my teaching. But I am not ignoring these behaviors. I usually wait until I can have some private time with the student and will deal with it then. By the way, one last thing: if I decide a consequence is warranted, it will be between the individual student and me and nobody else. I will not be sharing individual consequences with the entire class. Is there anything you don't understand?

After questions, give the students an example:

Here is an example of what I mean. I might drop by someone's desk [pick a student] and tell him to knock it off. As I am walking away, he might roll his eyes, deny doing anything wrong, or mumble something under his breath that is just loud enough for me to hear [It will never be "thank you for correcting me"]. Some of you might wonder if I heard him and what I am going to do about it. Trust me, yes, I heard it, and yes, I am going to do something about it—it just might not be at the exact time you all think I should.

Privately Praising and Correcting

Frequency: First day of school, early in the year, and repeated until they get it

Prevention phrase:

There are going to be many times this year that I drop by your desk, table, or workstation to deliver a message that is only for your ears. It might be something positive, or I might be correcting a behavior I do not like. After I do this, some of you might wonder what I said to the individual person. I just want to let you all know right now that I will not be sharing that message with the entire class. More than likely, I will drop by your desk this year just as often as I drop by everyone else's. Don't worry about what I said unless I was talking to you.

Differentiating Instruction

Frequency: Often—especially early in the year

Prevention phrase:

*Being **fair** means that every individual will get what he or she needs in order to be successful. Being **equal** means everyone gets exactly the same thing. I promise you I will always do my best to be fair to each and every one of you in this classroom this year. This means I guarantee you all right now I will not always be treating you exactly the same way. For example, you might get ten problems to complete, and your best friend in the whole world might only get five. I am not saying this* will *happen. I am just saying it* might *happen. And if it does, I do not want to hear anyone complain that I am not being fair. You might complain that I am not treating you equally, but I am not promising to treat you equally. I am promising to be fair.*

Giving Students a Say

Frequency: As often as you would like

Prevention Phrase:

Hey, everybody, I just want to let you know that I have been your teacher now for _____ [two weeks, six weeks, two months, and so on], *and I really, really, really hope you are enjoying my class and learning a lot. If you are not enjoying my class, if I am not being a good teacher for you, if there are ways I can make this class better for you, I want to share how you can let me know directly. My door is always open for you to tell me exactly what I can do to make this class better for you. Five to ten years from now, when someone asks you who one of your best teachers was, I want you to say me. Right now is the time to make that happen. I am not saying I will completely change the way I teach because some of you may not like my style. However, if you come and talk to me privately, there is pretty much nothing you can say to me that will get you in trouble. You can even tell me my teaching sucks* [naturally, use age-appropriate language]. *Of course, I might ask you to pick a more appropriate word. I might also ask for specific suggestions about how I can be better. But please do not hesitate to talk to me privately. If I do not hear from you, I will assume you are enjoying the class, are satisfied with how you are doing, and have no suggestions for how I can make things better!*

Many power struggles can be prevented by letting your students know how you will handle misbehavior if and when it occurs and assuring them that you will listen to and learn from them if they are unhappy with something you said or did. Since most kids who regularly invite power struggles are actually trying to have one or more of their basic needs fulfilled, prevention is primarily about implementing classroom practices that make students want to behave.

Prevention Strategies

Power struggles virtually always involve students with one or more of the unfulfilled basic needs mentioned previously: attention, power or control, competence, and belonging. Here, we take a look at specific strategies designed to prevent power struggles by addressing these basic needs. These prevention strategies include:

- In-class relationship building
- Outside-of-school relationship building
- Opportunities for students to be in charge
- Competence building

In-Class Relationship Building

Strong student-teacher relationships are vital to any well-run classroom and are critically important in effective behavior management. The degree to which students with challenging behaviors feel connected to the teacher strongly influences how they behave. Students might not like us all the time, but the goal is for them to always respect us. We have found it is easier to teach and influence people who like us than to teach and influence people who don't. Following are several strategies for building strong student-teacher relationships in the classroom.

Greet Students

We know this can sound very basic, but remember to greet students upon arrival. Say hello, and try to make eye contact with each student every day, by name or nickname, as they enter the classroom. Occasionally make a comment that reflects how you think a student's day might be going (for example, "You're looking good. Are you feeling good?" "Tough day so far? Is everything OK?" "You look like you have some things on your mind. If that's true, I hope you'll see me later or talk to someone else before the day is over.")

Keep track of birthdays, and bring in a card, cookies, or a small gift. Ask a personal but non-intimate question, and tell the student something about yourself. This can range from what you had for breakfast to sharing a hobby to mentioning something about one of your children. Be sure to do all of this casually. Naturally, if there is something that concerns you about the student, initiate the conversation as privately as possible. One of the best times to privately talk to students is when they are entering the classroom. It is easy to pull a student aside and say, "Hey, I saw your game last night. Awesome job. Get in there and sit down." Or, "Everything OK last night with your mom? I know when you see her on Monday nights sometimes Tuesday mornings are difficult. Was last night OK?" Hopefully the student will say everything was fine and you can move on to the next student walking in. If last night was rough, you might say, "I totally understand how you feel. If you want to talk about it sometime, I am glad to listen." This is what we mean by "personal" information. Remember, relationships are a two-way street.

Start With a Clean Slate

A teacher we know in West Virginia tells her students that each day they get a clean slate. This means that whatever happened the day before or with any other teacher is irrelevant to her. Students are expected to give her a clean slate every day as well. We have found that some students need a clean slate every fifteen minutes. Do not hesitate to adjust the timing to fit your individual situation with a student. Share a warm smile or, if necessary, a statement that turns the page from a tough moment that might have happened yesterday.

For example, "Wow Lakeisha, yesterday was a tough day for both of us, but today is going to be a lot better. Good to see you."

Seek Feedback on Your Teaching

Every once in a while, prepare your class as if you are about to give them a real test or quiz. At the last moment, have them take out a sheet of paper, and tell them they are taking a two-question quiz. Say the following:

Question 1: What are the best two things about me as a teacher?

Question 2: If you were able to press a button on me and change any two things about me, what would they be and why?

You can only get a 100 percent if all answers are complete, so be sure to answer each question.

This quick survey can provide great insights about how students perceive your strengths and what you can do to be an even better teacher. Sometimes patterns emerge. Do ten out of twenty students want to change the same thing? If so, you might want to look in the mirror and consider changing.

The next day, address the quiz results with your class. It should sound something like this:

Hey, everyone, I graded the quizzes, and you all got 100s, so awesome job. Thank you so much for telling me the things you think I do really well. I'll continue to do those things as often as possible. I did notice a pattern on what you would like me to change. Many of you think I'm a bit too demanding. In fact, one of you wrote, "Mrs. Yellin, it is 2:50 on a Friday. BACK OFF!" I totally understand why some of you feel this way. I know I come across as demanding sometimes, because I care a lot about making sure you guys each do as well as you possibly can. I prefer to call it being passionate, not demanding. Do any of you know what passionate means? Sometimes when a person cares as much as I do, her voice rises, her face turns red, and she just keeps pushing you to do your best even when we all need to chill . . . Do any of you get that way sometimes with things you feel strongly about? I will work on it because I'm definitely not perfect. Sound good? Once again, thanks for the feedback.

This concept can be transferred to many different parts of the school day. For example, you can ask what two things students love about school and what two things they hate about school.

There are other simple ways of keeping attuned to your students' interests and needs. Regularly ask your students to offer suggestions in a suggestion box about how the class can be more interesting or meaningful. Some teachers use the index-card method by asking students to regularly write down what makes it hard for them to learn and what helps them learn. You can occasionally give your students a more formal interest inventory such as the one in figure 1.

> **Regularly ask your students to offer suggestions about how the class can be more interesting or meaningful.**

Use the 2 x 10 Method

The 2 × 10 method is a great relationship builder. Choose one student with whom you currently do considerable battle or who you sense might be difficult. Make a commitment to spend two uninterrupted, undivided minutes of your attention each day with this student for ten consecutive days in an effort to build a different kind of relationship (for some students, it might be helpful to begin with one minute). You may ask any question, elicit the student's interests, or share your own during this two-minute sequence. You may *not* correct the student or in any way use this time to persuade the student to change his behavior or his mind about something. After ten days, assess the relationship. Most teachers who use this method have found that, initially, they do about 90 percent of the sharing with the student. By the end of the tenth day, there is generally a 50-50 give and take. Visit www.tlc-sems .com to watch a video clip of Brian Mendler demonstrating this strategy in a live seminar.

Eliminate the Phrases "I Need You To" and "You Need To"

Eliminate the phrases "I need you to" and "You need to" when correcting a student, and replace them with any of the following: "Thank you for," "I would appreciate it if," "Would you mind doing,"

Interest Inventory

Name: _____

Concerning this class, I am a person who . . .

likes _____

hates _____

can _____

cannot _____

would never _____

would rather _____

wants to learn how to _____

would be better off if _____

is really good at _____

gets angry when _____

bugs other people when _____

has the good habit of _____

has the bad habit of _____

wishes I could change the way I _____

wishes I could change the way other people _____

Outside of school, I am a person who . . .

never misses watching the TV show _____

will someday _____

enjoys going _____

can't wait to see _____

loves _____

can't stand _____

really wishes _____

Figure 1: Interest inventory.

"It would be nice to see," or "I trust you will." The goal is to talk to our students the same way we talk to other people in our lives. I cannot imagine saying to my wife, "I need you to do my laundry right now" or "You need to make me dinner" (and then slowly counting backward from 5 to 1 as if this will get her to oblige!).

Create an "I Am Good At . . ." Board

Have students bring in a picture of them doing one thing they are good at outside of school. On the first day of class, give each student two note cards labeled "A" and "B" with the student's name on them. On card A, the student writes down one thing he is good at outside of school. On card B, he writes one thing he is good at inside school. Then create a large bulletin board that says, "I Am Good At . . ." Put each student's picture on the board, along with the note cards telling what that person is good at. Now students can use the board before asking each other for help. For example, if Kristy doesn't understand multiplication, she can look at the "I Am Good At . . ." board and find someone to help her. In our experience, it's human nature to like helping people with things we are good at (and not like helping people with things we are not good at). Students helping each other can go a long way to prevent bullying and build a strong classroom community.

This strategy is also great if you get a new student during the school year. Before introducing the person to the class, have her look at the "I Am Good At . . ." board and pick out a few names of students she thinks could become new friends. For example, if Patricia is new and likes basketball, she can look at the "I Am Good At . . ." board to find others who enjoy basketball as well. Having something in common is so important for a new student. This also gives the teacher a structured way to introduce Patricia to students with common interests.

You can also use the board early in the school year when learning student names and interests. The board can be another tool for relationship building. You might actually put the board together after the first day of school rather than just explain it. Just be sure students bring pictures with them on the first day and you have a spot for the bulletin board. Again, do not be afraid to get creative and add your own ideas, experiences, and spin to this activity. A final idea related to this activity is for teachers to have an "I Am Getting Better At . . ." board, which can go next to the "I Am Good At . . ." board. This is for kids who are improving in different areas but might not yet be as good as they want to be. One caution: Some kids will not bring a picture. Be sure to have a camera ready in case this happens.

Outside-of-School Relationship Building

Since there isn't always time to focus on the importance of the teacher-student relationship during instructional time, the suggestions that follow are geared toward strengthening that relationship at other times.

Call or Text Students

Some teachers we work with have expressed concerns about calling or texting students, and some schools have policies against this practice. Nevertheless, when done properly, this type of communication can be very effective. We recently met a teacher in Nebraska who gathers all his students' cell phone numbers and sends a mass text reminding them of their homework, permission slips, and upcoming tests. Be sure to take a few precautions before making the call or sending the text:

- Tell parents you might occasionally call or text their or their child's cell phone. In fact, before you call a student, call the parent to let him or her know your intentions. Explain that you don't always have time to offer specific in-depth feedback during class that could help a student be more successful. Most parents will appreciate knowing you are concerned about their child. Be sure to respect parents who do not want you to call or text.

- Tell your students you might call them at home or send a text. This way, they are not completely caught off guard and panicked when the phone rings or beeps. Assure them that if you call, it will only be to share information that you think will help them be more successful in school.

- Stay away from texting personal messages of concern to avoid having your message be misunderstood or misconstrued.

- Use your judgment! A phone call home to a student should not last more than a few minutes. If it looks like it might take more time, arrange for a meeting at school, or let the parents know the nature of the conversation you want to have. If the topic is sensitive, it is best to avoid discussion on the phone.

Attend Extracurricular Activities

Attend games, plays, recitals, and any other meaningful events students are doing outside of school. It is more important to be seen than to see. Find your students, and make sure they see you at the event. Make eye contact, wave, or, if you can, personally greet them. If you have the time to stay through the event as a show of support, that would be great, but if you don't, leave when students are focusing on the event. Remember, it is important for you to see your students, but it is much more important for them to see you! The next day, talk to the students about the event and how they did. If you had to leave early, just be sure to ask the coach what the final score was and a few things about the game.

Volunteer

Set up volunteer opportunities with your students and then participate. Special Olympics is one of several organizations always looking for volunteers. You might even try to find an event during the school day. A teacher we know in Olean, New York, does a Special Olympics field trip every spring. All of her students, along with about six staff members, volunteer with baseball, softball, track-and-field, and award ceremonies for the athletes. Some difficult students have spent their entire lives being helped. Putting them in a situation to help others is often a powerful strategy for improving behavior.

Invite Students to Attend Events

Ask students and their families or friends to attend your events outside of school, or at least tell them about different events you are participating in. For example, if you are in a recreational sports league, participate in a community orchestra, or play in a band, invite your students to come and watch. If you volunteer at a soup kitchen, invite them to join you. If you are having a family picnic, consider inviting a few of your students who may rarely have this opportunity, or you can sponsor an outdoor barbecue early in the school year for your students and their families. If you notice a community event in the paper that you plan to attend, and that might not usually draw their interest, let them know. For example, if you see a 5K walk or run, challenge them to join you in participating. As always, use caution and judgment when being a part of students' lives outside of school.

Visit Students at Home

Go to students' residences to say hello or see how they are doing. Apply the precautionary principles listed under "Call or Text Students" to in-person visits. Stopping by to see a student who is sick, suspended, or a constant disruption can go a long way toward getting him or her to comply upon return. Even one home visit can be a powerful way of communicating how much you value that child's presence. Bring along some school work that the student might have missed and offer support and instruction. Seeing a child in her own surroundings can give you a better idea of her interests, hobbies, and influences. This can provide you with a great opportunity to get to know her better and to help her get to know you. If you have concerns about being alone with the student or anxiety about going into the community alone, ask a colleague to accompany you. We recommend always making sure a parent or guardian is home and present at all times during this visit.

> Even one home visit can be a powerful way of communicating how much you value that child's presence.

Opportunities for Students to Be in Charge

The best way to address the need for power or control and to teach responsibility is by providing opportunities for your students to make decisions about issues that affect them and then acting on those decisions.

Create Classroom Jobs

Students with challenging behaviors are often surprisingly conscientious when they are given the opportunity to be responsible. For example, a school in Baltimore has a student ambassador program. The job of an ambassador is to welcome new students to the school, give them a tour, and share such things as rules and procedures. Some of the most difficult students in the school make the best student ambassadors. Ambassadors are expected to display a high standard of performance and behavior in order to maintain their positions. All classes, particularly at an elementary level, have many functions aimed at filling the need for power and control that can be performed by students. A few of our favorites include:

- Passing back ungraded papers
- Being on "bully patrol" and looking out for bullying in different parts of the school
- Inspecting hallways or bathrooms for cleanliness
- Being a noise monitor
- Greeting visitors when they come into the room
- Asking students to provide questions for tests or quizzes
- Supplying materials to students when they forget a pen or pencil
- Asking students for ideas about an art project or a story to read
- Asking students for ideas about classroom tasks or activities they think they should be responsible for

It is only necessary to have a chart letting the entire class know what each person's job is if doing so gives students a feeling of power and control or creates a structure that can be helpful to everyone.

Assign Responsibility for Pets or People

Students who seem to care little about others (those with low empathy) need opportunities to positively bond with others. They need experiences that teach them how they can affect others in positive ways. Since many students desperate for power and control have spent their entire lives needing help, it can be quite powerful to reverse that by putting them in charge of helping, mentoring, or nurturing someone or something. Some students are empowered by learning that they can make a positive difference in the lives of other living things. Caring for pets, being a big brother or sister for a younger child with problems, or partnering with senior citizens in need at a nursing home are just a few examples of empowering new situations. Since many of these students have a history of being verbally, sexually, or physically abused by others, they need to be supervised while participating in these kinds of activities. Consider connecting with a teacher of younger students so that you can pair your students who need to be helpers with students who could benefit from having an older, wiser friend.

Organize a One-Week Positivity Campaign

Students with challenging behaviors make themselves hard to like. It is as if they practice inventing new ways to turn people off. As educators, we have to become better at refusing to reject students than they are at triggering rejection. Spend one day observing a student who really irritates you. Work hard to find some redeeming positive quality that you might build on. If you struggle to find something, try thinking of a behavior you usually find annoying, and identify what is positive about it. For example, a "defiant" student could be thought of as "opinionated" or "independent." For the next week, be certain to affirm this positive quality at least once each day. For example, try seeing a hyperactive student as energetic and think of ways you might put him in charge of leading the class in a physical activity. Tell him, "Jamil, you are really good at jumping, but sometimes you get into trouble when we are all supposed to read. Today we are going to do reading and after ten minutes, I am going to ask you to lead the class in twenty-five jumping jacks. You can demonstrate the proper form, and then walk around helping others that are not quite as talented as you. Can I count on you to stay quiet during reading and then lead us?"

Defer to Student Opinions

This strategy can be a powerful way of affirming a challenging student. Model respect to all students by deferring to the opinion of a difficult student when an opportunity presents itself. If a student asks a question about something, when possible, say, "Go ask Meg about that. She's good at _____." When students hear their teacher respond with respect, they are more apt to respond in kind. Use the "I Am Good At . . ." board to help with this.

Find and Connect With Classroom Leaders

Most classes we have taught or observed have between one and three student leaders. These are the kids who set the tone and can exert their influence in a positive or negative way. If you can change the student leaders, they will change the class. Build relationships with them first. If you concentrate on gaining influence with them by building a relationship, you will often be able to count on them to influence others. It should not take long to figure out who they are. In most classes, it will be obvious. If you are not sure who they are, here are some things to look for:

- After giving a request, who does everyone look at?
- When X is absent, do you seem to have a much better day?
- In elementary schools, who do students want to sit by at lunch?
- In middle and high schools, who are the good athletes?
- Which students seem popular?
- Who is not afraid to yell, "Shut up!" to the entire class and usually gets others to quickly comply?

Here are some phrases to begin getting leaders on your side:

- I am really proud of how you did _____.

- I saw your _____. I really liked it.

- When I was your age I did that, too, so don't worry. But here is what you can do instead.

- What has the day been like so far? Because today I am going to need everyone to really concentrate. Do you think you can help get and keep everyone else quiet? I sure would appreciate it.

- I like your _____. Where did you get it?

- Did you know they all like to follow you? You are a great leader.

- Since everyone follows you anyway, can you please help me _____?

Some teachers might feel like giving a misbehaving, disruptive student all of this power is inappropriate. We totally understand that thought process, but remember, the other kids already know how much power these students have, as they exert it every day.

When you know you will be absent for a day, tell the leaders you will be looking to them to help keep things in check while you are gone. For example, you might tell them you will be calling them the next night to hear how things went, and you expect a positive report.

Ask Them to Help Make Some of the Rules

People who lack real power and influence are much more likely to break others' rules as a way of asserting their need for control. This can often be countered by giving your students opportunities to make or revise classroom rules. You might even consider having them propose possible consequences should rules be broken. Be sure to maintain final decision-making authority since students are much more apt to be punitive than instructional when thinking about consequences. As the teacher, take primary responsibility for identifying and explaining the values that are necessary for student success.

We like to tell our students, "Respect is extremely important this year in this classroom because what we say and do, and how we accomplish this, affects how successful we are. For example, if someone gives a wrong answer and you say 'That was stupid' or you roll your eyes, do you think that student is going to be more or less likely to answer a question again? There are lots of ways to show respect. Who has some ideas about rules we need to follow to make sure we show respect?"

It is also important to teach students exactly what rules and values are. Rules should always be specific and definitive. Values are broad and general. Rules tell students *what* to do, and the value explains *why* they are doing it. For example, the value of "safety" is important when driving a car on the expressway. The speed limit is sixty-five miles per hour (rule). The value tells why it is important to follow a rule. This is the best way to know if you have a bad rule. If the answer to "Why do I have to follow this?" does not tie to a value, we recommend possibly eliminating the rule. "Because I said so," "Because that's the way it has always been," and "Because I do not feel like changing it" are not values!

Allow students to have input when it comes to rules.

Take time to allow students to have input when it comes to rules and you will take another major step in preventing the power struggle storm.

Tell Less, and Ask More

Pick a day during which, from the time you arrive at school until the time you leave, you respond to anything anyone says to you with a question. For example, if Debra says, "Mr. Davidson, that's not fair!" Mr. Davidson would answer, "Really? Do you have a way I can make it better?" When it comes to challenging comments a student makes, answering a complaint or a "trap" question (such as "When are we going to ever use this?") with a question (such as "What are all the things you plan to do in your whole life?") empowers the student by putting the responsibility right back on the student, which is exactly where it belongs.

Competence Building

When students believe they cannot be academically successful, they are much more likely to either shut down or act out. There are numerous ways that we can keep them involved and productive by making it difficult for them to fail.

Respect and Teach to Different Learning Styles

Schools are for teaching and learning. Based on Gardner's seminal work in the identification of different types of intelligence, Slavin (2009) has found that people have at least nine distinct intelligences—spatial, verbal/linguistic, logical/mathematical, bodily/kinesthetic, musical, interpersonal, intrapersonal, existential, and naturalistic—yet only two are being emphasized in school. The two that receive the greatest emphasis are (1) verbal/linguistic and (2) logical/mathematical. You and your students can check out the website http://literacyworks.org and individually fill out a self-guided assessment tool to get a sense of your and their intellectual strengths and what they mean. It may be that a preponderance of behavior problems comes from students whose strengths lie mainly in one or more of the intelligences that are not being emphasized in school.

There are many different ways to teach content. Do not be afraid to get away from the monotonous textbook and lecture formats. Here are some ideas to help improve content:

- Do a project or give assignments that involve students interviewing other people. When students learn how people are using or developing information, that information gains personal relevance.

- Take field trips to places or sites of study. Often, you may not have to go far. We recommended to a teacher in Colorado that she occasionally teach earth science outside. We observed her using a textbook to teach about mountains with the Rockies directly in sight from her window!

- Act things out. Make the material come to life. Give students the most important content, and have them create a song, skit, or debate that will help everyone else learn the concepts.

- Let students draw or build objects related to the curricula content. Many students love to use their hands. Some will use them to build things, while others will use them to punch someone if they aren't given a more constructive outlet. You decide which is better.

- Make collections, then compare and contrast. Noted educator John Goodlad (1994) found that students tended to learn concepts better when they collected examples of the concept being studied. For example, you might have students collect leaves from different trees, words that all mean the same thing, or objects that have more or less resistance to gravity. The tangible objects allow for much greater recall later on when the student is tested or quizzed.

- Give choices within an assignment. It is often sufficient to give students the proper structure and let them create ideas or express their knowledge independently. For example, you might give an assignment with the following choices: write an essay, create a rap, or draw a picture that includes at least three causes of the Civil War.

- Use movement. A math teacher in Pennsylvania takes her students to the gym to do graphing. She uses lines on the basketball court as the x and y axis. For example, if she says, "Johnny, -4, 3." Johnny has to move left four spots and up three. Each student does this until a line is formed. Instead of watching the teacher graph, they are actually doing it! She also uses the lines to teach angles, such as greater than and less than.

Use Creative Tests, Quizzes, and Homework

Once in a while, allow students to use their notes on tests or quizzes. A teacher we know gives a wild card question on all tests and quizzes. Students can put a line through any question they do not want to answer. In its place, they need to write and answer a question they wish she would have asked about the content. The goal is for kids to do well and start feeling capable. Success breeds confidence, and confidence breeds success.

A math teacher in Omaha told us this story. Privately, she asks a student to complete one problem for homework. Then she gives him the answer to that problem and tells him to check his answer against hers. The next day in class, he does the problem on the board in front of everyone. Getting it correct in front of everyone makes him feel good about school. The next day, she gives him two problems. This time she only gives him one answer. She tells him to do the other on his own, but to get to class early the next day so she can check it. If it is not correct, he only does the problem she helped him answer.

Use an Index Card for Note Cramming

Allow students to fill a 4 × 6 note card with as many notes as possible before a test or quiz. When filling up the card, students are studying the material while simultaneously deciphering the most important information. Each student is allowed to use the card on the test. Some classes might use a 5 × 7 card. It is up to you!

Help Students Identify and Develop Their Talents

We believe that every individual has a talent or skill. However, some students have no idea what their talent or skill is. Try hard to help your students figure out their talent, and then help find a way to utilize it. I (Brian) used to work with a student named Geoff who did absolutely nothing in class. He always had his head down and never participated. One day he was walking out of my room and a piece of paper fell out of his notebook. I picked it up to see one of the most incredible sketches I have ever seen. That afternoon, I asked the art teacher to talk to Geoff about being a part of the drawing club. This young man ended up graduating from college and is now a graphic artist. Remember to include traits such as persistence, effort, determination, and independent mindedness when noticing and developing talents. Try to connect the trait or skill in a way that could provide service to others or with something the school needs. It is so important for kids to find something productive to be a part of.

Be Happy With Improvement

Emphasize effort and improvement instead of dwelling on where students should ultimately arrive in their learning outcomes. Be happy with where they are as long as you see continued growth in all areas. Challenge your students to compete against themselves by being a better reader today than they were yesterday. Try to create lessons, assignments, and a grading structure within these parameters as much as possible. This is actually the number one way to improve test scores and decrease drop-out rates. On a daily basis, compare kids in all aspects of school to themselves instead of each other. Yesterday Billy read two paragraphs. Today it needs to be three or more for an "A." Yesterday Christina called out inappropriately six times in class. Today it needs to be five or less! We know this can be a difficult concept for teachers to grasp because of the extreme focus on "raising test scores." But if the grade-level criteria for success is a three-paragraph essay and some of your students can barely put together a three-word sentence, then lessons and assignments must be changed to accommodate that student. Watch drop-out rates decrease as well when utilizing this system. When students just need to be better today than they were yesterday, many see hope where there never was any.

Are You Causing or Contributing to Discipline Problems?

Following is a list of teacher behaviors that are frequently mentioned as contributing to well-run classrooms with few discipline problems. This can serve as a self-evaluation checklist. We advise rating yourself on each of the following using a scale of 1 to 5 (where 1 means almost never, and 5 means virtually always). If you experience frequent conflict with one or more students, you might ask a trusted colleague to observe, rate, and discuss as well. You might even consider having your students rate you for the purpose of getting feedback from them.

1. The teacher does a great job moving and mingling with students at the beginning of class.

2. The teacher has an enthusiastic, engaging, and strong voice.

3. The teacher is not easily sidetracked by one student's irrelevant question.

4. The teacher is interested in her students and teaches content by using student interests.

5. The teacher greets and shows a personal interest in students.

6. Concepts are clearly taught and clarified, and the teacher is patient when students do not understand something.

7. Questions and learning objectives are easily understood and prominently displayed.

8. The teacher is not tied to any one style of teaching and often adjusts to accommodate students at different levels or abilities.

9. When a student asks a question, the teacher encourages student involvement in answering.

10. When the teacher asks a question, he gives time for students to think about the answer before calling on someone.

11. The teacher uses current events to help promote her lesson.

12. The teacher almost never leaves any "down time" in his class.

13. The teacher cares more about her students than the subject matter.

14. It is obvious that the teacher is passionate about his content and works hard to invent creative lessons.

15. The teacher gives students numerous opportunities to be successful in her class.

16. The teacher makes requests and answers questions in a respectful, dignified way.

Add your own items to this list.

_____

_____

_____

_____

_____

Questions for Reflection to Help Prevent Power Struggles

The questions that follow may help you identify and prioritize strategies that can prevent power struggles.

1. When you visit a friend's home, what are some things he or she does that help you feel welcome? Can you apply these in your classroom?

2. Identify at least three practices you can do in the classroom without changing your basic style of teaching to promote a sense of connection with your students.

3. What responsibilities can you assign to your students to give them a sense of importance in the classroom?

4. What values do you believe are necessary for good learning and teaching to occur (for example, respect, courteous listening, absence of verbal harassment)?

5. After you identify these values, in what ways can your students develop or modify classroom rules and consequences to reflect each of these values?

6. When teaching each lesson, can you make the goals of the lesson clear to yourself and your students? What do you expect students to learn by the end of the lesson? A common challenge of students is to ask why they need to learn what is being taught. Aside from the fact that it might be on the test, work to help them understand how the learning is likely to provide benefits either now or in the future. If you cannot identify any real benefit, but you are required to teach the content and they are required by the school, district, or state to learn it, then let them know that it is likely to be on a test you did not create but that they will need to pass in the future.

Intervention Strategies

While prevention practices are usually effective because they address the unfulfilled basic needs that drive misbehavior, some students persist in challenging authority. Their needs are too strong to be managed by prevention strategies alone. Sometimes intervention strategies are needed.

When students present challenging, button-pushing behaviors, it is important that we respond to them respectfully while preserving our own dignity. We must remind ourselves that we are professionals, and at the end of the day, the only people we can truly control are ourselves. Just as a doctor wouldn't normally yell or kick out a patient who is bleeding all over his office, we need to do our best to maintain professionalism in the midst of crisis. This is definitely easier said than done. We have four tips to help in these situations:

1. Stay connected to kids without taking what they do and say personally.

2. Understand the hostility cycle.

3. Substitute less powerful words and images for those you find disturbing.

4. Reframe the situation.

Stay Connected to Kids Without Taking What They Do and Say Personally

A major key in working with misbehaving youngsters is staying personally involved with them while refusing to take personally their obnoxious, irritating, or threatening behaviors. Again, this is not easy, and it requires that we stay in complete control of ourselves at all times.

In his pioneering work with troubled youth, Fritz Redl (1966) spoke about the importance of adults being able to manage their counteraggressive impulses toward hostile children. It is important to recognize that troubled students will make you mad; many are experienced in getting people to dislike them. Realize that most kids with chronic authority issues lack trust because they have been purposely or inadvertently hurt by caretakers they have come to count on. Many will then test caring adults by showing their worst behaviors until they are convinced that the tested adult will not stop caring about them even in the face of distasteful behavior.

Permit yourself to honestly and privately express the frustrations you are likely to feel during these periods of testing either with a trusted friend or the school counselor/psychologist. In fact, we recommend teachers have a "calm corner" in a part of their room. Consider including some sponge-material squeeze balls or overstuffed pillows for students to take out their frustrations without hurting themselves or others. The teacher should monitor this, but as long as nobody is in danger, he should allow the student some freedom to release her emotions. It is important to take good emotional care of yourself at all times. Quick stress relievers like deep breathing, forward and backward counting, listening to relaxing music, and taking a brisk walk can help. You will also need to take periodic vacations from such students. A "sick of kids day" is warranted once in a while! Develop a support network with colleagues that enables you to separate yourself from the student for brief periods. We know some teachers who use each other for temporary time-outs. They send students with challenging behaviors to each other with a certain pass that signals their need for a short break from the student. Let the student know that you are at least as stubborn as he or she, with an approach that says, "I know the game. You want to do everything you can to push me away because then you will prove yet again that everybody and everything is unfair. But I am not going away, so get used to me."

So now you may be asking yourself, this all sounds great, but what if I use these strategies and the student is still out of control? Good question. Intervention strategies are designed to get challenging behaviors to stop so the teacher can get back to the lesson as soon as possible.

Questions

1. What methods can you use to keep yourself calm? From the strategies mentioned, which ones might work best for you?

2. What are three specific strategies your closest colleague uses when he/she feels stressed or frustrated?

> **Intervention strategies are designed to get challenging behaviors to stop so the teacher can get back to the lesson as soon as possible.**

Understand the Hostility Cycle

We know that children who view the world in a hostile way provoke hostility in others. When their action achieves the hostile reaction they are looking for, it provides evidence that the world is a hostile place (fig. 2 illustrates this phenomenon; see page 41). The only way to break the cycle is for adults who are "regulars" in the lives of the student to refuse to feed the cycle.

A few years ago, I (Allen) was working with a group of delinquent youth. It was our first meeting. Midway through the session, Dale glared at me, made a clearing noise with his throat, and spit directly into my face. He smirked at me and asked what I was going to do about it.

Remembering the hostility cycle was not what jumped into my mind. In fact, remembering what we are supposed to do in times of crisis is not always easy.

So, with spit on my face, I glared at Dale and assertively said, "Do you have a tissue?"

Caught off guard, he hesitantly said, "No, I ain't got no tissues."

I nodded at him, got a few tissues, removed my glasses, and wiped my face. I said firmly, with teeth clenched, and with more than a hint of anger, "Dale, I guess I have been lucky in my life because that was the most disgusting thing anyone has ever done to me. But it sickens me to think that you have so little respect for yourself that you would do such a thing. You are better than that!" I then walked toward him with the disgusting tissue and handed it to him while saying, "I think this belongs to you."

Later on when the meeting had ended, I met with him individually and said, "Dale, you and I are new to each other and need to find a way to coexist. The state says that you and I need to meet in order for you to qualify to leave this place. There is no doubt we will both say things the other does not like. If you ever say anything to me that pisses me off, I guarantee that I will never spit in your face. I respect myself and you too much for that. Can I also expect that if you ever get mad at me again you will find another way of expressing it? Even though I do not know much about you yet, I believe that you have too much respect for yourself and others to spit in people's faces. I would greatly appreciate you using words to tell me what I did that made you so mad. Do I make myself clear? Now what was it you were trying to say?"

Dale was not an easy kid to work with. However, he and I began to form a bond, and he never spit in my face again. In fact, he began seeking me out during his free time and even asked me to help him practice what to say when someone made him mad. He confided in me that he was tired of getting in trouble and, deep down, really wanted to change but had no idea where to start. By understanding the hostility cycle, we give ourselves the opportunity to model exactly what we want students to do when someone does something inappropriate to them.

Questions

1. Have you ever had someone you don't really trust try to be nice to you? How did you react? Your reaction or anticipated

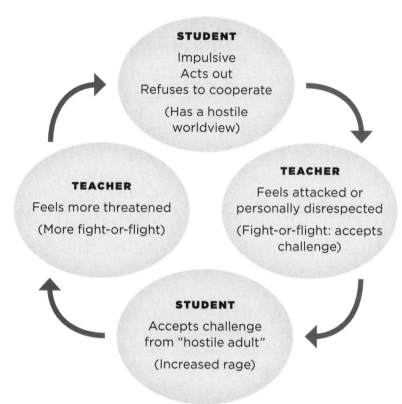

Figure 2: The hostility cycle.

reaction is probably similar to how some of your untrusting students feel toward you!

2. Using the hostility cycle graph in figure 2, think of one student with whom you often have power struggles. Write down what the student says or does that triggers a hostile response from you. How do you usually respond? How does the student respond to your reaction? How does it usually end? Can you see how the hostility cycle is at the root of power struggles? You will shortly learn many new ways to handle these triggers.

3. What words can you use to replace the word *hostility* within the same cycle?

Substitute Less Powerful Words and Images for Those You Find Disturbing

To get beyond a fight-or-flight response when you get angry, it is first necessary to neutralize the attack. We can successfully accomplish this by substituting less powerful words and images for those we find disturbing. The examples that follow provide illustration.

1. **The student uses inappropriate language.**
   Imagine the student said something that wouldn't bother you. What if they said "hat" instead of the offensive word? Your initial reaction would likely be very different. Hearing the word differently or "changing the channel" will often give you the buffer you need to not automatically react when you feel your buttons getting pushed.

2. **The student uses an inappropriate gesture.**
   Imagine a student raised his pinky to the side rather than his middle finger straight up. If you can visualize this, you might even be able to raise your pinky back at him. You are letting him know it is just a finger, and you value all five on each hand equally.

Reframe the Situation

Remember, any student who is misbehaving in school is most likely learning these behaviors or having them reinforced through experiences with other role models in his or her life. We do not always know where the behavior comes from, but we know it is there. Home life is often a good place to start looking for the source of behavior problems. This is important to remember because students with challenging behaviors make themselves so resentful that it is hard to see them as anything other than an annoyance. While providing new pictures or words for difficult situations can help us remain calm, a final step is to provide a new interpretation of the student's behavior and then respond. The entire process is called *reframing*. It can be a powerful way of regaining a sense of personal control so we can go back to the drawing board and begin to rethink ways of best reaching a challenging student. It is a key way of staying personally connected to the student without taking offensive behavior personally.

Power struggles can often be either prevented or reduced through reframing. If we view a driver on the highway who cuts us off as an inconsiderate, dangerous madman, chances are good that we feel frustration and anger. But if we discover that the driver was racing to the hospital after learning of a serious accident involving his child, we view the same behavior very differently. In an objective sense, there is no excuse for behaviors that endanger others, but how we choose to interpret the incident powerfully influences our reactions.

We suggest practicing reframing several times before attempting to make a reframing statement. Otherwise, it can come across as sarcastic. Rehearse and role-play in private, and implement only when able to do so without sounding sarcastic. Also realize that you may or may not actually say or do these things in response to the student, but the feelings and energy reframing creates will often enable you to influence the student's behavior more effectively.

Following are four typical discipline problem behaviors and a way of reframing each.

1. **The student is late to class.**

   Many teachers get upset with students who are late, and getting to class on time is certainly desirable and should be encouraged. However, the good news is that the student came to class. Reframing requires that we see coming late as preferable to not coming at all. An example of a reframing statement is to say, as privately as possible, "Bill, I am disappointed that you are late again, but coming late is better than not being here at all. I know it takes effort to get here. I just want to say that you are an important student in our class, and we miss you when you aren't here. So let's try to figure out how we can see even more of you." Reframing requires conveying the attitude to the student that he or she is more important than his or her behavior. It is important to set a limit by expressing disappointment and even by implementing a consequence (such as requiring the student to stay late), but the emphasis in reframing is highlighting the person's relative strengths (no matter how minimal) to solve the problem.

2. **The student has a temper tantrum.**
   The good news is that nobody got hurt. Relatively speaking, Sally exercised decent self-control. A reframing statement in this scenario might be, "Sally, do you know that when you got really mad this morning, you showed good self-control. Even though you knocked over a chair and used words that are against the rules, you didn't hurt anyone. That was good. How did you remember to remind yourself not to hurt anyone? Let's look at how you might do an even better job next time you get mad."

   Successfully implementing this approach requires an attitude from the educator that says, "You are more important than what you do, although poor choices usually have consequences." Do not be afraid to ask the student if she has any ideas for a consequence that will keep her from throwing a tantrum in the future. Sometimes the best ideas come directly from our students.

3. **The student talks excessively to others.**
   The good news is that this child is socially connected. His presence also gives others an opportunity to learn how to work with distractions present. An example of a reframing statement in this situation is, "Ben, I really like that you are not afraid to speak out loud in front of others. But I bet you've noticed that people have one mouth and two ears. Am I right? I think your two ears can learn a lot from your mouth. Do you think when other people are talking, your mouth can quietly talk to your ears and remind them to listen as well as your mouth talks? Let's give that a try." Practice through role-play could follow this conversation.

4. **The student puts her head down on her desk.**
   When a student has her head down, pretend she is visualizing possible questions on the state exam. If you had that

thought, might you not respond differently than thinking she is bored or being disrespectful?

Questions

1. What behaviors occur in your classroom that you find objectionable?

2. Which students show these behaviors regularly?

3. What are positive benefits either to you, the class, or the offending student? For example, if a student does no homework, you have one less paper to grade (benefit to you), which means you can give more time to the papers that were turned in on time (benefit to others). In a sense, the student has donated his time to his classmates. Furthermore, that student is probably struggling to retain his sense of pride since he doesn't want to be reminded that he is stupid (if he can't be successful) or weak if he caves in to authority (benefit to the offending student).

4. Can you imagine the student is in front of you? How can you express the benefits of his objectionable behavior without sounding sarcastic? Repeat the process until your words and beliefs are compatible. This often takes a long time because we are unaccustomed to noticing positive aspects of behaviors we find objectionable.

A Reframing Activity

People accommodate change more readily when they do not feel forced to let go of the familiar. Instead of forcing a student to give up a familiar behavior, try implementing a new behavior that can fulfill the same need alongside the familiar one until the familiar one is no longer necessary. Following are opportunities to practice and apply reframing.

1. Identify a chronically irritating student.

Instead of forcing a student to give up a familiar behavior, try implementing a new behavior that can fulfill the same need.

2. Identify the problem behavior and what you believe is the root cause of the behavior (behavior—calling out; reason—seeking attention).

3. Identify at least two positive aspects of the behavior. Relatively speaking, what is acceptable about the student's behavior? How do you, the class, or the student benefit (he wants to be involved, and he sometimes has interesting things to say)?

4. Imagine the student is in front of you; try to express these benefits genuinely. You may also express your displeasure and/or give a consequence, but you must first highlight the benefits. (Desmond, when you call out, it lets me know you want to be involved, and many times you have some very interesting things to say. I wish everyone was as eager as you. But I need to hear from others also, and when you call out, it doesn't give other students a chance to answer. I know we have talked about this before, but so far, talking about it hasn't solved the problem. Can you think of some consequences that you think will best help you remember?)

5. Implement the strategy with a student who shows excessive inappropriate behavior—especially after you have tried more conventional strategies.

Defusing Strategies

When students are behaving in a way that interrupts the teaching and learning process, actions need to be taken to effectively end the problem moment. Using defusing strategies increases the likelihood that the problem will end, while still keeping the teacher in control. In this section, we look at the goals of defusing, basic defusing skills, and a defusing activity with specific statements that will help defuse tension with tough kids in the moment. We will also provide additional steps that may be necessary when dealing with the rest of the class and show you specifically how to follow up with difficult students.

Goals of Defusing

There are five goals that are helpful to keep in mind when defusing a power struggle: (1) treat students with dignity, (2) preserve dignity for yourself, (3) keep the student in class and get back to teaching, (4) become a next-to-last-word person, and (5) teach an alternative to aggression.

Treat Students With Dignity

It is hard to treat students with dignity when they behave unacceptably. A true professional educator responds to displays of misbehavior with disapproval while still respecting the student. We believe that part of our job is to treat all students with dignity and respect.

To do less invites hostility and retaliation. Remember, tough kids have tenure. If they leave feeling humiliated, they will be back to get even tomorrow!

Preserve Dignity for Yourself

It is equally important that we preserve our own dignity when under attack. The teacher must be able to assertively stand up so that she is not viewed by others as being weak. This is why the prevention phrases discussed earlier (page 11) are so important. Start predicting the behaviors before they come. The key when your buttons are being pushed is to locate a response that enables you to stand up without fighting back.

Keep the Student in Class and Get Back to Teaching

Power struggles are almost always about the same thing. The student does not want to look bad in front of his friends, and the teacher does not want to look bad in front of the class. So the argument begins. It often goes back and forth until the teacher removes the student. There are times when a student is so out of line that it becomes impossible to teach or for other students to learn. At these times, a trip to the principal or a colleague for a time-out may be appropriate. However, frequent disciplinary referrals elsewhere diminish the adult's authority. It signals that the adult in charge is unable to handle a difficult situation. Worse, it does nothing to model a realistic solution to a challenging interpersonal problem that the students who witness the incident can apply in their own lives. For example, no student is able to order another student to the principal's office! In addition, the student's absence puts him behind academically, creating a problem for the student and more work for the teacher. The next section focuses on what to do instead.

Become a Next-to-Last-Word Person

Most adults in our culture have learned that when there is an argument, the person with the greatest authority gets the last word. This seems especially true of teachers. Think about your own life. My father insisted on the last word, and in raising my children (including Brian), so did I. Recently, Brian's wife told him, "Brian, you are such a last-word person." As he walked away he said, "No, I am not!" She smiled. With difficult students, we need to be different. Be satisfied with the most *effective* word, and with difficult students, this will often come next to last. It is that final "whatever" that so many difficult students need in order to save face. Really work hard to not engage the student at that point. If you walk away, the power struggle almost always ends, and later you can talk with the student if you feel that is necessary.

Try hard to retrain your brain to become a second-to-last-word person with tough kids. This will get you out of almost any argument or any power struggle that comes your way. Allow your last word to be "thanks," and then get out of there. Move. Do not stick around. For example, say, "I believe I saw you drop that piece of paper, and I would appreciate it if you would pick it up. Thanks." GONE. The student will mumble and grumble about you under his breath. Let him. Usually, the power struggle stops here because the teacher is no longer engaged. Remember the prevention phrase "Following Up Later" (page 11), which is very important to this concept.

Teach an Alternative to Aggression

How we respond to conflict is a critical element in either gaining or losing credibility with our students. With many schools establishing peer mediation and conflict-resolution programs for students, we believe it is necessary for adults in charge to model the very strategies they want students to exhibit. When a student calls a teacher an inappropriate name, the incident actually provides the teacher with an opportunity to show students how to stand up to conflict effectively without either caving in or fighting back. These moments provide important reinforcement of conflict-resolution programs, because students see an important adult using a skill that the school is promoting for students.

Basic Defusing Skills

With the above attitudes in mind, the strategies that follow will enable you to effectively defuse most power struggles quickly in a dignified way that preserves your authority and redirects the energy of the class (including the offending students) back to the lesson.

Privacy, Eye Contact, and Proximity

Before things career out of control, most potentially difficult power struggles can successfully be solved by the educator giving his corrective message to the student with privacy, eye contact, and proximity (PEP). Successful use of PEP requires that the teacher frequently circulate the room while teaching so that he is in close natural proximity with all students throughout the day. This makes it possible to blend corrective messages with those that are appreciative. Both praise and correction should be done as privately as possible. Publicly praising often annoys and aggravates the students not being praised. Publicly correcting usually prompts a defensive response.

When using PEP, try hard to get as close to the student as possible, make direct eye contact, and deliver a message quickly and directly. Some students will not make eye contact for cultural and emotional reasons, while others may get overwhelmed with anxiety when you come close. In these cases, don't push the eye contact, and maintain more distance (at least one arm's length away). As soon as the message is spoken, get out of there. Do not stick around for a response. Speak quickly, directly, and firmly, and then move right into something else. When this strategy is used effectively, a teacher can both compliment and correct the same student within a few minutes. The prevention phrase "Privately Praising and Correcting" (page 12) is very important to this strategy.

> **When using PEP, try hard to get as close to the student as possible, make direct eye contact, and deliver a message quickly and directly.**

The movement part (walking away) is so important to making this work. When all students know that a regular part of the teacher's behavior is making frequent private contact with each student for purposes of giving feedback, it is rare that student defensiveness will occur when being corrected. Make sure to privately praise and correct the same student. Otherwise, the teacher becomes predictable. Remember, a big reason for power struggles is the student's desire to seek status among his peers, and drawing the teacher into public battles is a favored method for achieving status.

Nonverbal PEP

Index cards and sticky notes provide an alternative to verbal forms of PEP. Separate cards or notes can say such things as "thanks," "way to go," "please chill," or "stop." Cards or notes can also use pictures or colors such as a stop sign or a green or red traffic light. Nonverbal PEP is delivered the same way as its verbal brother. Drop or flash the card privately, and then get out of there. Other sayings with pictures can easily be created (see fig. 3, page 53).

Listening, Acknowledging, Agreeing, Deferring

When a student is more agitated or challenging, we suggest a process involving listening, acknowledging, agreeing, and deferring (LAAD). Skillful use of one or more of these components is extremely effective in defusing a power struggle. Let's take a typical situation that can easily blow up to show how these skills can be used. When Luis's teacher asks him to open his textbook, Luis loudly tells her, "You can't make me." A power struggle is likely to occur if the teacher accepts the challenge (for example, by responding, "Yes I can," "I'll call your home," "That is no way to talk to me," or "Get out!"). LAAD provides a sound alternative.

Listening

Hear what the student is saying, not how he is saying it. Listening requires that the person receiving the message hears either the words or the mood of the speaker and feeds that understanding back to the speaker before returning to the lesson. Usually, a simple nod is all that is needed while quickly redirecting back to the lesson.

Acknowledging

Let the student know you hear him. "Luis, if I understand you correctly, you feel strongly against opening your book and are telling me that you are not planning to do what is asked. Am I right about that?" Either students will shift their behavior at that point and comply (since they got the attention they sought) or they will say "Yeah." If the latter, conclude with "Thanks for letting me know." Acknowledging can be done with words or actions. A knowing look can serve the same purpose. Attention should be redirected to the lesson immediately after the acknowledgment. Notice how the teacher does not argue with Luis. This is important. Acknowledge without criticism, opinion, or argument.

Agreeing

Let the student know that what he is saying is or might be true. This is by far the hardest step for most teachers. Allow yourself to struggle with it at first. It sounds like this: "Luis, I guess you are right about that. I cannot make you do things. Only you can make yourself. I will be here if you decide help is needed. Good luck." Once again, get out of there physically, and then get back to the lesson as soon as possible. Agreeing is powerful because it acknowledges the real control the student has and puts the responsibility right back where it belongs.

Deferring

Let the student know specifically when you will address the issue. The goal of this step is to let the student know a specific time you are willing to discuss his concern or problem. You might say, "Luis, if this continues, we are going to have an argument in front of everyone, which makes both of us look bad. We can avoid that right now and talk right after class. Thanks for your cooperation." If the student doesn't stay after class but stopped his inappropriate behavior and seemed to get your point, let it go. Saying what you said and doing what you did was enough to stop the behavior. Offering an option to continue exploring the student's concerns at a time when it is possible to provide adequate attention is often effective in defusing a continuation of the power struggle. On the other hand, if you feel a need to follow up with a discussion or consequence, meet with the student after class, and take care of business then.

Figure 3: Sample PEP cards.

Keep in mind that with all of the strategies offered thus far, the primary goals are to keep the student in class and get back to teaching and learning without escalating the problem.

Verbally Acknowledging Power Struggles

Most students who have continued to this point will stop when you acknowledge that a fight or argument is about to break out. Let the student know it is important to both of you to avoid looking weak: "Sue, I see it one way, and you see it differently. I can see we're about to have an argument over this, and I know that neither of us likes to lose. We'll talk more later. Thank you for waiting." Get back to teaching.

Offering the Door, but Inviting to Stay

When a student's behavior persists at interrupting the teaching and learning process, it may be time for a temporary time-out either in the classroom (for younger students), in a planning room, or in the office. The student is essentially offered a last chance: "Sue, I need this to stop right now, or I need you to leave. Even though I'm getting angry, I hope you choose to stay because you are an important member of this class, but I'll understand if you need to go. If you go, come back when you're ready, but I hope you can stay." Then get out of there and get back to teaching.

Giving Temporary Control

If the student continues, there is no help available, and the student is making it impossible to continue teaching, you can usually regain control by letting it go temporarily. Approach the student, hand over a piece of chalk, and say, "Sue, I can't continue. Why don't you teach for the next few minutes? You're in charge. Anything goes except class dismissed!" You may choose to sit in a seat as a student and do some role reversal. When you sense that the student is running out of steam, get up, go over to the student, take the chalk, and continue on with the lesson.

Deciding if Consequence Is Necessary

Whether or not any of the previous actions succeed in ending the problem moment, you still need to decide on a consequence. A consequence should be given if you can see how the problem student will learn from it or if you feel you must take some visible action for purposes of showing the other students that following rules is important. For example, if the behavior was dangerous or blatantly disrespectful, you will want to send a message both to the offending student and to all other students, explaining that an important line was crossed. In these cases, a visible consequence like detention or suspension is usually warranted.

In the event a decision is made to give a consequence that is apparent to others, it must be done in a dignified way. For example, after class, the teacher meets Sue and says, "Sue, I'm sure glad we were able to stop our argument. I appreciate that. I know you were angry, but saying what you did to me is just never OK. Not only do I want you to remember to follow the rules, it is important that other students realize that saying certain things—even in the heat of the moment—will not be tolerated. For that reason, I will be writing a referral and strongly suggesting that you have detention for the next few days unless there is something else you can think of that might make more sense." The teacher can then either give the consequence or develop a consequence with the student based on the student's input.

Consequences work best when given privately. All students may know that a consequence has been or will be given, but they do not need to know what it is or hear it expressed.

A Defusing Activity

Write down things that students say or do that trigger anger in you and make you want to fight back. Some common examples include the following:

- "Go ahead, you think I care?"
- "NO!"

- "You're not my mother!"
- "I don't have to."
- "This class is boring."
- "This class sucks!"
- "Why do we have to do _____?"
- "Whatever."
- "F___ you, b_____!"
- "What are you going to do about it?"

Are there any others that you experience? Are there any nonverbal behaviors that students display that seem designed to annoy or anger you? Add to our list.

_____

_____

_____

_____

Imagine a student is now displaying one of these behaviors. Using one or more of the statements that follow, practice writing and then saying a statement designed to defuse the student.

Here are some specific statements to defuse power struggles early and quickly (every example assumes the teacher moves away from the student after the statement is made):

- I'm disappointed that you are choosing to use such angry words, even though I am sure there is much to be upset about.

- I am really concerned! It is very important that I understand why you are so mad. Please tell me later when I can really listen. Thanks for waiting.

- Your words/actions tell me you are bored. It takes a lot of discipline to hang in there when you are unsure about why we are doing certain things. Thanks.

- I know you are angry, but there is no problem so big that it can't be solved. Do you need a time-out right now, or can you use your words to solve the problem?

- You're just not yourself today, and that must feel lousy. Let me know if there is anything I can do to help.

- We both know there are other ways of telling how we feel while still being respectful. Please share your thoughts with me after class.

- Throwing chairs doesn't make problems go away. It only creates new ones. What do you think you can do to express yourself differently next time?

- I really want to understand what I did to annoy you, but swearing at me does not help. Let's talk later when we can figure this out.

- Wow, you must be feeling awfully mad to use those words in front of everyone.

- Are you trying to embarrass me/yourself by saying/doing that? It makes me want to fight back, but then we'd never solve the problem. Let's talk about this later.

- I'm glad you trust me enough to tell me how you feel, and I'm concerned. Any suggestions for improvement are appreciated. Please leave them in the suggestion box.

- There may be some truth to what you are saying, but if you really want me to hear you, there is a more respectful way to go. When would you like to discuss this?

Notice how these defusing statements acknowledge the behavior but try to move the discussion to a later time. Both are so important.

Practice the following defusing statements:

1. Picture the challenging student right in front of you.

2. Pick one of the defusing statements, and say it while trying to use a tone of voice that conveys firmness *and* respect. Be sure to actually say it out loud rather than just thinking it. The words work only when conveyed with the right attitude.

3. Practice that statement at least five times (much more repetition may be necessary since breaking old habits and acquiring new strategies can be difficult).

4. Pick another statement if the first doesn't seem to fit, and repeat.

5. Continue as needed.

6. Find another colleague who is struggling with a student. You won't have to look very far. Take turns role-playing behaviors and responses with one person as the teacher and the other as the student, and then switch. If you can find a third colleague, we recommend video recording the interaction and watching it later. Evaluate each other and yourself.

1. State the rule and possible consequence using PEP.

2. Ignore the hook.

3. Use listening and acknowledging.

4. Use agreeing and deferring.

5. Verbally acknowledge there's a power struggle happening.

6. Offer the door, but invite to stay.

7. Give temporary control.

8. Decide if a consequence is necessary.

Challenge Strategies

Students who regularly challenge authority have three primary purposes: (1) they are attempting to have influence in their lives, (2) they are protesting oppressive limits imposed by others, and (3) they have little if any direction or structure and are looking for boundaries. Oppositional students view threats and consequences as invitations to feel powerful. They will often argue just for the sake of arguing. Telling a student "I know you can do it" or "You better do it or else" usually backfires because he always has to prove the opposite of what the teacher says. In addition to the relationship-building strategies discussed earlier, the best approach we know to use with these students is called the "challenge strategy." It is especially effective with students who do not respond favorably to praise and other forms of positive reinforcement. To warn you, this will sound very different from the conventional strategies most of us learned in our training.

It is also contrary to much of what we have taught in this book. But in order to be effective, we believe you need every possible tool. This is one that will be rarely used. However, when used effectively, it is a fast behavior changer.

Almost everyone likes a challenge as long as they believe the challenge can be successfully accomplished. If the ability to succeed is not there, the challenge strategy will only lead to annoyance and frustration. When challenging a student, we are basically saying, "I am not sure you have the ability to succeed. I guess we will see." Remember, this only works if a student really does have the ability. Here is an example of how to use the challenge strategy to get students to behave better when you are gone (for instance, when you have a substitute). Say this to the entire class:

> *Hey guys. I just want to let you know that I will not be here tomorrow. I am taking the day off to attend a workshop. I want to let you all know right now that I trust you will behave when I am gone. I look forward to a great report when I get back.*

Then as they are walking out of the room, pull the leaders aside and say this:

> *Hey, real quick. You know what I just said to the entire class about them behaving tomorrow when I'm gone? Well, actually, I lied. I don't care how they behave. I really don't. You see, the only two names I am looking at when I get back are the two of you. You guys are able to get everyone to follow you all the time. Of course, we all know you can lead them in a negative way. But I'm not so sure you can lead in a positive way. I don't know if you have the ability to help get everyone quiet. I guess we'll see. I also don't know if you really have the ability to help get everyone lined up for lunch. I guess we'll see about that, too. I look forward to reading the report when I get back.*

We are not saying this approach will always get them to behave or get them to influence others to behave. However, many students will do the right thing just to prove you wrong. And when it happens, do not get excited. Instead, say,

> *Well, yeah, I am proud of what you were able to do when I was gone, and thanks for helping influence others. But seriously, anyone can behave and lead in a positive way for one day. I have my doubts about your ability to keep it up for a full week, though! But don't worry. Not everybody is as tough as they think.*

Are you getting this? After a week your message becomes:

> *Who can't behave for a week? I will be really proud and excited after a full month. But I am not so sure you are capable of that. I guess we will see.*

Following are several challenge phrases you can adapt to your classroom:

- Yesterday you did three problems. That's good. I'm not so sure you can do all five tonight, though. I guess we will see.

- Great job with your reading homework. But I don't think there is any chance you will complete it two nights in a row! Good luck, though!

- I know you behaved today, and that really is great. But I would be much more impressed if you acted the same way tomorrow. I am not sure you have it in you. Good luck!

- I am not so sure you even have the ability to lower your voice. Do you?

- Just about anyone can get others to be mean. Getting others to be nice to _____ by inviting her to lunch would take real leadership. It makes me wonder if you really have what it takes.

- You did a really good job behaving on the field trip, and I am proud. But do you think you are able to behave that way on the next field trip? I am not so sure. I guess we will see.

I hope you are able to see why challenge works so well. Difficult kids are constantly threatened about what will happen if they don't do certain things. For the most part, it makes them mad, and their goal becomes showing the teacher the very opposite of what is expected. I (Brian) am a big believer in this strategy because it is what motivates me. Throughout my life, starting in school, there have been people who have doubted my capabilities. Nothing makes my blood boil more, which usually inspires me to work hard to prove that person wrong.

> **Difficult kids are constantly threatened about what will happen if they don't do certain things.**

The Private Three-Step Approach

When a student persists in displaying the behaviors we've been discussing, the "private three-step approach" is an effective method. This is a good strategy to use with a chronically difficult student who consumes considerable time.

When alone with the student, use three statements conveyed in a respectful and assertive manner. Let's suppose that Lee has been verbally offensive several times. The three-step approach works as follows:

1. **Use an "I" message.**

   "Lee, when you use those words in class, I get upset, disappointed, and even embarrassed."

   Be sure the "I" does not precede "need you to"—remember, per page 18, to avoid that phrase.

2. **Use the "I must have done" phrase.**

   "I must have done something to make you really upset, and if I have, I'm sorry, but we need to work it out. Please let me know if you have any suggestions for how I can keep from making you so upset next time. Thanks for your input."

3. **Take a problem-solving approach.**

   "What did I do that made you mad? Did you contribute to the problem? What can we do together to work things out?"

A Private Three-Step Approach Activity

Think of a student who regularly does something that bothers you. Identify a time that you can have a private discussion with the student. Use the three-step approach.

It is important that you speak these words slowly, with good eye contact (unless the student won't offer it due to either cultural or emotional reasons), and in a firm yet respectful manner. We have found that approximately 90 percent of all students respond positively to this type of intervention.

Student Removal and Follow-Up

Sometimes a behavior is so bad that it warrants removing a student from class. We continue to emphasize that this should be our last option. The goal of every competent and caring educator should be to make it really, really, really hard for a student to throw away her education. Unfortunately, that is exactly what happens when a student gets thrown out of class. However, once in a while, removal is necessary. In those cases, removal should be done in a way that gets the student back to the classroom as quickly as possible by conveying that she is an important member of the class and will be missed if she leaves. Here are the two times when removal virtually always becomes necessary:

1. The student is physically violent toward the teacher or another student.

2. Things are so bad that the teacher literally cannot teach.

That is it. No other time. So if a student comes to class late, is chewing gum, or stands instead of sits, is that grounds for removal? No. By applying these two criteria, we are immediately able to decide if the behavior warrants removal. If not, the teacher can focus all energy on figuring out what to do instead of removing the student. If the student does need to be removed, we recommend offering the door instead of kicking them out. It sounds like this:

> *You know what, Marisol? Your behavior has been so rude, so nasty, and so out of control that I cannot teach anymore. Do you see the door over there? If you need to go, feel free to go. I would prefer that you stay and behave yourself because you are an important part of our class, and I will miss you if you are gone. If you go, come back as soon as you are ready to learn. But right now, I cannot teach, so go if you need to.*

Notice we did not throw the student out. In fact, we did not even demand that she leave. We set a clear, firm limit, but we also provided a choice: leave, or stay and behave yourself. We also told her she was important, we would miss her, and to come back as soon as she was ready to learn. If she stops and stays, find a way to privately thank her for her cooperation. If she leaves, welcome her back warmly and optimistically when she returns.

Student Suspensions

If a student is suspended, a phone call home to the suspended student can do wonders to deepen or repair the relationship. Call and say this:

> *Hey, Russell, it's Mrs. Oliver. I have no idea what happened today, and I don't want to hear the whole story about why you*

are suspended. However, I do want to let you know that I wish you were here. You are an important part of my class, and I don't like it when you are out. If, for some reason, you decide you do not want to be further behind when you get back, just let me know, and I will find a way to get your work to you.

This next part is optional but extremely powerful:

If your parent or guardian is there, I will bring your work to your house. And if they stay, I might even stay for a bit and help you finish it. If you want, I can ask your other teachers if they have work as well. If not, that's OK, too. Just thought I'd offer. I'm looking forward to seeing you when you get back.

This one phone call that takes no more than thirty seconds is so effective. Now when Russell comes back and Mrs. Oliver asks him to take off his hat, he will. But when another teacher who can't get beyond the traditional methods asks him to take the same hat off, he will tell her where to stick the hat. It is not about the hat. It is about how last week, when he was suspended, one person tried to help him, while the other preferred his absence. Perhaps the phone call works so well because very few teachers do it. It is much easier to be there for students between the hours of 7 and 3:30. Separating yourself from the other teachers takes going above and beyond. Since most educators don't think to reach out to suspended students, those who do often gain stronger influence because the student feels cared about even though he has done something unacceptable.

It is extraordinarily important that we refuse to give up on difficult students. A bad day needs to be followed by a welcoming attitude on the part of the teacher. We cannot afford to lose any of our students. When suspended or expelled, they become the problem of our communities. So it is in our long-term interest to keep at it, even though it is unlikely we will be shown much—if any—appreciation in the short term. It can be helpful to remember the saying "all students have tenure." Say something like,

Bob, we had a rough day yesterday. It was tough for both of us. Welcome back today. I know it's going to be better.

If you occasionally lose it with a student in front of the class and probably contributed to embarrassment, do not be afraid to apologize. This is a great opportunity to show all of the other students what remorse looks like and how to express empathy. Say,

Bob, your behavior made me mad, and I think I am owed an apology. But whether or not you apologize, it wasn't right for me to go off on you and embarrass you in front of the class. I am truly sorry. Welcome back!

The Rest of the Class

Many teachers fear that if one student behaves a certain way, many others in the same class will behave that way too. We call it the copycat effect. And there is certainly an element of validity to this concern. In fact, in our experience, rarely will more than 25 percent of kids want to act like the disrupting student. The good news is that at least 75 percent will not. This concern too often leads to an escalating get-tough response, which fans the flames.

As the professional, it is absolutely essential that the teacher refrain from falling prey to this phenomenon. It is usually necessary to stop and think before acting. We are continuously trying to promote this idea to students, and it is therefore necessary that we model it. The old-fashioned suggestion of "walk the talk" is particularly relevant here. The teacher must stand up to the assault without fighting back. She must present herself as capable of stopping the problem, while preserving the dignity of the student and herself. Accomplishing these goals is achievable in most cases. Use of the defusing strategies shared earlier (page 47) is one approach. Another is to deal effectively with the rest of the class. To do so, we encourage teachers to be honest with their students.

Immediately after a challenging incident has occurred, it is common for other students, either verbally or nonverbally, to wonder what the teacher is going to do about it. We encourage teachers to anticipate this reaction by saying something like,

I know you all just heard what LeShon said, and I'll bet most of you are wondering what I am going to do about it. So I am going

Concern for the rest of the class can be met by:

- Defusing the power struggle by using one of the statements suggested earlier in the Defusing Activity (see pages 55–58)

- Acknowledging that a challenge occurred (for example, "Most of you probably heard or saw what was said or done.")

- Safeguarding your dignity and the challenging student's dignity (for example, "You're probably wondering what I'm going to do about it. In all honesty, I need to first find out why the student is so upset that he's doing something that is against the rules.")

- Using humor (when possible)

- Redirecting class attention to the lesson (for example, "Let's get busy with _____.")

- Reminding yourself to include strategies of prevention to meet the basic needs that drive misbehavior when these needs are unfulfilled.

- Firmly telling students that they need to worry about themselves and not be concerned about what you, the teacher, are doing for other students in the class.

- Have fun. Enjoy the rest of the class. So often one or two students dominate our attention. This is not healthy for anyone.

to be up front with all of you. The answer is that I have no idea what I'm going to do about it because I have no idea why LeShon is so upset today that he needs to use language that all of us, including LeShon, know is inappropriate. So when LeShon and I have some time to figure this out, I'm sure we'll come up with a proper solution [consequence]. *This will be the last time I discuss what LeShon did with all of you. Whatever happens from now on will be between him and me and nobody else. Sound good?*

Honesty, preservation of dignity, and humor can often help defuse the situation and buy time until a more thoughtful solution can be found. Even if a challenging student stops challenging after the teacher gives a response, it may still be necessary to give a consequence to the student for reasons already noted. Just be sure to reiterate to the entire class that whatever consequence is decided on will be between that individual student and the teacher.

Finally, remember that effective discipline in a group situation focuses on prevention. Show students with challenging behaviors that they have influence by welcoming them and asking for their opinions. Invite them to join in developing classroom rules. Expect them to behave, and hold them accountable when they don't.

Power Struggle Scenarios

Now it is your turn to practice using what you have learned throughout the book. Read the problem situations that follow, and decide what strategies to use. Or better yet, we suggest writing your own real-life situation and then practicing it with colleagues. Getting really good at dealing with difficult kids is like any other skill in life: it takes a lot of practice and hard work. You might prefer working collaboratively with colleagues on these scenarios while including role-playing, discussion, and brainstorming. It is never a bad idea to video yourself and then watch it later for both learning and laughs!

1. Nancy is working, and her teacher begins to pass out papers to other students. She gets agitated for no apparent reason and exclaims, "This class is stupid!"

2. A teacher asks a child to stop running in the hall. The student doesn't stop.

3. Ryan raises his hand to answer a question in class. His teacher calls on another student. Ryan slams his hand down on his desk and yells, "I'm done raising my hand. You never call on me."

4. Mistie continually blurts out answers without raising her hand.

5. Ben regularly leaves his seat to visit others during work time.

6. Julio refuses to work in a cooperative group.

7. Than makes faces at other students to annoy them during class discussion.

Two Stories

Instead of us telling you what to focus on in the following stories, we would like you to draw your own conclusions.

Deacon

I (Brian) recently met a preschool teacher who told me about a four-year-old, Deacon, who was obsessed with guns. He drew guns, built guns with LEGOs, and talked about guns. Her efforts to prohibit such play were met with even more intense, aggressive play. She was understandably concerned that other children would become aggressive and was trying to promote an atmosphere of cooperation and nonviolence.

When I asked her if she knew much about this child's background with guns, she dejectedly told me that Deacon had seen his cousin killed, and his uncle was the recent victim of a drive-by shooting that took place in his home. Deacon was in the next room when this happened. It was clear from the discussion that this young child was stressed, frightened, and preoccupied with these events and was reliving some or all of this through his play. In effect, he had no other place to turn for safety and meaning than to his play.

His teacher needed help seeing that to give this child a sense of control, she needed to find ways of engaging his need for guns in his play. She was encouraged to do a lot of active listening by following the themes he was setting. For example, as he was drawing a picture of a gun, she began to say things like, "Guns can sometimes be scary—especially when they hurt or even kill people we love." Deacon needed to be engaged by someone who cared and was able to decode the message. He needed to know that she would do everything in her power to make sure he felt safe in the classroom. Eventually, his preoccupation diminished, at least temporarily, though the absence of a strong emotional support network made his eventual outcome far from certain.

With so many children experiencing major crises on an almost daily basis, we must reframe our concept of the classroom to include affirmation and validation of their real-life experiences, even if they are very different from our own. Since wounded students who externalize their pain often project it onto those who are closest, we need to be prepared for their expressions of anger, torment, frustration, and humiliation. While Deacon confined his aggression to gun play in the classroom, many other students target their peers or adults.

It is easy and natural to either fight or run when under attack. Making a difference with such students requires that we do neither. The needed response is for us to stand up without fighting back. It is to let the student know that we find his or her behavior objectionable, but that we are able to push beyond it while, at the same time, preserving our dignity and providing a positive example for a classroom full of shocked, wondering students.

The major challenge when students elicit feelings of counteraggression in us is to find ways of staying personally involved with them without personalizing their misery. We must realize that students who attack are virtually always under attack. If attacked back, the never-ending cycle perpetuates itself. Since such students see the world as a hostile place, they often set others up to reject them so their worldview will be confirmed. When we continue to care and refuse to give up, it is common for them to push harder and harder until, finally, they surrender to the possibility of bonding. Continuing to care is no easy process, but it is wonderfully rewarding at the end of the road.

We must realize that students who attack are virtually always under attack

Jimmy

I (Allen) recall Jimmy, who was seven years old when I first met him in his second-grade classroom. Frequently out of his seat, aggressive with others, and easily angered, Jimmy's patient, capable teacher often sought support. A network of support staff in collaboration with her efforts helped Jimmy get through that year and the next few.

I lost contact with him for a few years, but I met him again when he was in seventh grade. By that time, Jimmy was even more troubled and disruptive. All of his teachers knew him as a troublemaker by the second week of school. When I asked him if there was any-thing at all positive about school, he eventually told me that he "kinda" liked his English teacher. As I asked for details, Jimmy said, "She understands kids, and she lets us tell it like it is." Somewhat guardedly, he told me that because of her he was becoming a poet. At my request, Jimmy brought a stack of poems into my office the following day. Most of them were written on torn paper and used napkins. I could not put them down; they revealed the inner work-ings of this troubled boy:

> *I feel like stone*
> *Solid and cold*
> *As the bread that is so old,*
> *Like ice which hurts to the touch*
> *It fills my heart with pain too much*
> *Where is the comfort I need to survive*
> *Where is the hope to keep me alive*

I couldn't help but realize that this student who was negative, nasty, and defiant to most of the outside world had such depth of feeling. Working effectively with such students requires that we look beyond the obvious and respond. The hope for this boy was in his teachers, and now, years later, Jimmy is in college studying to be one! In his words, he is succeeding because some of his teachers "refused to give up on me despite my best efforts to get them to throw in the towel!"

Adapted from Mendler, 1995.

Final Thoughts

It is important to recognize that troubled students will make us mad. They will get to us because they are experienced in getting people to dislike them. We must allow ourselves to honestly and privately express these frustrations. We need to take good emotional care of ourselves in order to hang in there. We must let the student know that we are at least as stubborn as he is by using an approach that says, "I know the game. You want to do everything you can to push me away because then you will prove yet again that everybody and everything are unfair. But I am not going away. I know you've got worth even though you may not think you do." If need be, do more than suggest this through your actions; say it directly to the student.

It also is necessary to prepare for power struggles. Students will test our resolve, dedication, patience, and persistence. Dealing with these students requires great courage and much skill to stand up without fighting back. Most problem moments can be defused through a combination of listening, acknowledging the student's concern, agreeing that there may be some truth in the student's accusation, and deferring to a private time for continued discussion. In our work with delinquent youth, we often have noted that their most prized possession is a teddy bear or some sort of stuffed animal. It was at first shocking and saddening to watch teenage boys sleep behind a locked door, clutching their teddy bear in a near-fetal position. We must remember that these tough kids are emotional infants! They need nurturing *and* limit setting.

Finally, it is important that we not castigate ourselves when we occasionally do lose our cool. Like a champion prizefighter, success requires endurance and the strength to suffer an occasional knockdown. Remember, the school year is 180 days for a reason—it takes time to change and grow. Many of the students we talk about in this book did not become the way they are overnight. Do not expect to change them overnight. Allow the process to work, and be proud of small accomplishments you make on a daily basis. It is educators like you who make this world a better place for all of us to live. Keep up the great work, and thanks to all of you for never, ever, giving up!

References and Resources

Armstrong, T. (1999). *7 kinds of smart: Identifying and developing multiple intelligences.* New York: Plume.

Curwin, R. L. (2003). *Making good choices: Developing responsibility, respect, and self-discipline in grades 4–9.* Thousand Oaks, CA: Corwin Press.

Curwin, R. L. (2006). *Motivating students left behind: Practical strategies for reaching and teaching your most difficult students.* Rochester, NY: Discipline Associates.

Curwin, R. L. (2007). *Rediscovering hope: Our greatest teaching strategy.* Bloomington, IN: Solution Tree Press.

Curwin, R. L. (2010). *Meeting students where they live: Motivation in urban schools.* Alexandria, VA: Association for Supervision and Curriculum Development.

Curwin, R. L., Mendler, A. N., & Mendler, B. D. (2008). *Discipline with dignity: New challenges, new solutions* (3rd ed.). Alexandria, VA: Association for Supervision and Curriculum Development.

Gardner, H. (2006). *The development and education of the mind: The selected works of Howard Gardner.* New York: Routledge.

Goodlad, J. I. (1994). *Better teachers, better schools.* San Francisco: Jossey-Bass.

Langer, E. J., & Rodin, J. (1976). The effects of choice and enhanced personal responsibility for the aged: A field experiment in an institutional setting. *Journal of Personality and Social Psychology, 34*(2), 191–198.

Mendler, A. (1995). Classroom counteraggression. *Reclaiming Children and Youth: Journal of Emotional and Behavioral Problems, 4*(1), 16–17.

Mendler, A. (2000). *Motivating students who don't care: Successful techniques for educators.* Bloomington, IN: Solution Tree Press.

Mendler, A. (2001). *Connecting with students.* Alexandria, VA: Association for Supervision and Curriculum Development.

Mendler, A. (2005). *MORE what do I do when . . . ? Powerful strategies to promote positive behavior.* Bloomington, IN: Solution Tree Press.

Mendler, A. (2006). *Handling difficult parents: Successful strategies for educators.* Rochester, NY: Discipline Associates.

Mendler, A. (2007). *What do I do when . . . ? How to achieve discipline with dignity in the classroom* (2nd ed.). Bloomington, IN: Solution Tree Press.

Mendler, A., & Curwin, R. (1999). *Discipline with dignity for challenging youth.* Bloomington, IN: Solution Tree Press.

Mendler, B. (2009). *The taming of the crew: Working successfully with difficult students.* Rochester, NY: Teacher Learning Center.

Mendler, B., Curwin, R., & Mendler, A. (2008). *Strategies for successful classroom management: Helping students succeed without losing your dignity or sanity.* Thousand Oaks, CA: Corwin Press.

Redl, F. (1966). *When we deal with children selected writings.* New York: Free Press.

Slavin, R. E. (2009). *Educational psychology: Theory and practice* (9th ed.). Boston: Allyn & Bacon.

Wood, M., & Long, N. (1991). *Life space intervention: Talking with children and youth in crisis.* Austin, TX: PRO-ED.

Index

A

acknowledging students, 51–52, 54
aggression, alternatives to, 49
agreeing with students, 52
anger, handling. *See* intervention strategies
attention-seeking kids, 8

B

belonging, 10–11

C

calling students, 21–22
challenges
    copycat effect, 65–67
    phrases to use, 61
    private three-step approach, 61–62
    reasons for, 59–60
    suspensions, 63–65

classroom, keeping students in a, 48–49
clean slate, 16–17
competence, 10
    building, 29–32
consequences, deciding on, 55
content, methods for improving, 29–30
control, giving students a sense of, 9–10, 54
copycat effect, 65–67
corrections, privately giving, 12

D

deferring, 52
defusing
    activity, 55–58
    goals of, 47–49
    skills, 50–55
differentiating instruction, 13
dignity
    student, 47–48
    teacher, 48

Discipline With Dignity for Challenging Youth
Allen N. Mendler and Richard L. Curwin
Create positive change in your most challenging students with the help of proven, practical strategies found in this resource.
BKF229

Motivating Students Who Don't Care
Allen N. Mendler
Spark enthusiasm in your classroom with proven strategies and effective processes to reawaken motivation in students who aren't prepared, don't care, and won't work.
BKF360

What Do I Do When...?
Allen N. Mendler
Understand the principles that place dignity at the core of classroom management, explore what motivates misbehavior, and learn strategies for making a positive impact on schoolwide discipline.
BKF230

MORE What Do I Do When . . . ?
Allen N. Mendler
Counter negative student behavior with positive actions that preserve dignity. This resource provides 60 powerful, proven strategies for reaching challenging students.
BKF231

P

positive qualities, looking for, 25–26

power, giving students a sense of, 9–10

power struggles
preparing for, 5–7
scenarios, 69–72

praise, privately giving, 12, 50, 53

prevention strategies
competence building, 29–32
in-class relationship building, 15–21
outside-of-school relationship building, 21–23
reflection questions, 34–35
student empowerment, 24–29

privacy, eye contact, and proximity (PEP), 50–51

private three-step approach, 61–62

R

Redl, F., 38

reframing situations, 42–46

relationship building
in-class, 15–21
outside-of-school, 21–23

Rodin, J., 9

rules, student proposals, 27–28

S

Slavin, R. E., 29

Special Olympics, 22

stress, handling, 38–39

student
dignity, 47–48
empowerment, 13–14, 24–29
opinions, 26
removal of, and follow-up, 62–63
suggestion box, 18, 19
suspensions, 63–65

T

talents, identifying and developing, 31–32

talking, handling excessive, 44

teacher behaviors that contribute to misbehavior, 32–34

teacher dignity, 48

teaching, feedback on your, 17–18

temper tantrums, handling, 44

tests or quizzes, use of creative, 31

texting students, 21–22

time-outs, 54

2 × 10 method, 18

V

verbal defiance, forms of, 6

volunteer opportunities, 22